Gateway 1
Activity Book

Jeanette Greenwell
Stephen Lawrence

Garnet
EDUCATION

Published by
Garnet Publishing Ltd.
8 Southern Court
South Street
Reading RG1 4QS, UK

This edition first published 2010
Reprinted 2011
ISBN 978-1-85964-594-9

Production
Project managers: Edición Integral AdLib, S.C. Mexico
Editorial Consultant: Fiona McGarry
Editorial team: Edición Integral AdLib, S.C. Mexico
Design: Aphik, S.A. de C.V.
Illustration: Hugo Miranda Ruiz & Laura Castillo Cervantes
Photography: ClipArt, Corbis & Lorena Campa

Printed and bound
In Lebanon by International Press: interpress@int-press.com

Gateway 1

Activity Book

This book belongs to:

_____

School: _____

Grade: _____

Group: _____

Roll number: _____

Table of Contents

Introduction

1. Read, match and color.

Hello! My name's Sam.

My name's Kiko.

Hello! My name's Mandy.

My name's Velvet.

Unit 1 · The Bakery

Lesson 1

1. **Ask and answer.**

Hello! What's your name?

My name's Tom.

Hi! What's your name?

My name's Timmy.

What's your name?

My name's _____.

2. **Read and trace.**

How are you?

I'm fine, thanks.

1. Match and complete.

What's his name?

What's _her_ name?

What's _____ name?

What's _____ name?

Her name's Mandy.

His name's Kiko.

_____ name's Sam.

_____ name's Velvet.

2. Look and write the numbers in the speech bubbles.

2 – Good morning! 4 – Good afternoon!

3 – Good evening! 1 – Good night!

1. Look and draw a line.

• Say and trace the words.

2. Look and draw the candles.

3. Complete the questions and the answers.

1. How old is   she ?

   She's _____.

2. _____ _____ is he?

   He's _____.

1. Label the picture. Use the words in the box.

| clap ✓ | look | open | jump | close | sit down | listen | stand up |

clap

Do or mime the actions in Exercise 1.

I can ...!

Greet People

Greet Velvet.

_____ !

Hi!

Tell People My Name and My Age

Draw and write about yourself.

My name's _____ .

I'm _____ .

Ask and Answer About a Person's Name and Age

Draw and write about two friends.

What's his name? _____.

How old is he? _____.

_____? Her name's _____.

_____? She's _____.

Give and Follow Commands

Read and do.

Stand up   Clap   Sit down

Count and Write from One to Ten

Circle the number that comes first.

3 / 1   7 / 5   2 / 4   8 / 10   9 / 6

Write the number words in order.

_____   _____   _____

_____   _____   _____

_____   _____   _____

_____

Unit 2

Do and Share!

Make a name card for your desk.

You need:

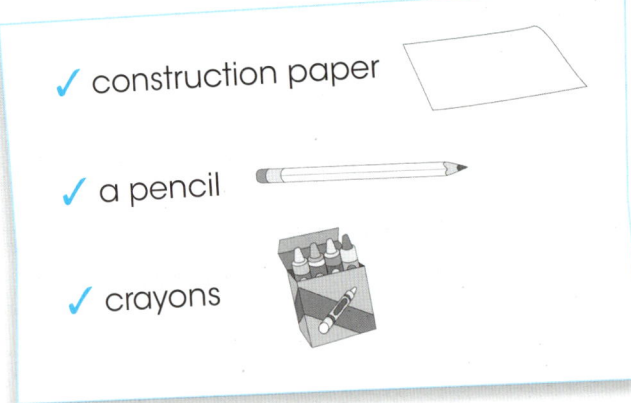

- ✓ construction paper
- ✓ a pencil
- ✓ crayons

1. Fold.

2. Draw.

3. Write your name.

4. Fold again and show it to your group.

My name's Ray. I'm six.

Go to Unit 2!

Unit 2 · The Pet Store

Lesson 1

1. Find and number.

1. snake	6. spider
2. fish	7. dog
3. mouse	8. bird
4. cat	9. ant
5. owl	10. lizard

  1

2. How many ...

letters in 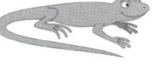 ? _____

letters in  ? _____

letters in  ? _____

letters in  ? _____

3. Guess the words.

___ p ___ ___ ___ ___

___ ___ t

d ___ ___

___ i s ___

___ ___ z ___ ___ ___

4. Look, say and spell.

1.  ☐ ☐ ☐

2.  ☐ ☐ ☐ ☐ ☐

3.  ☐ ☐ ☐

4.  ☐ ☐ ☐ ☐ ☐

5.  ☐ ☐ ☐ ☐

1. Circle *a* or *an*.

1. (a)/ an   fish   3. a / an   ant   5. a / an   snake

2. a / an   owl   4. a / an   bird

2. Color the correct sentences.

1.
It's a fish.

It isn't a fish.

3.
It's an ant.

It isn't an ant.

2.
It's a snake.

It isn't a snake.

4.
It's a dog.

It isn't a dog.

5.
It's a mouse.

It isn't a mouse.

3. Unscramble the letters. Complete the questions and answers.

1.
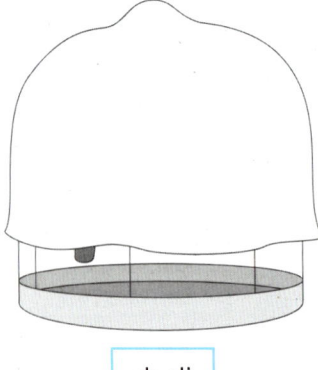

rbdi

What is it?

It's _____.

2.
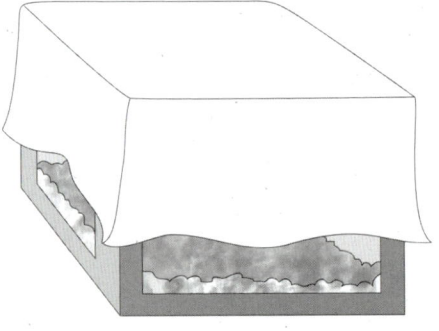

eskna

What _____ _____?

_____.

Lesson 3

1. Match the questions and answers.

1.  Is it a spider?

2.  Is it an ant?

3.  Is it an owl?

4.  Is it a snake?

5.  Is it a cat?

6.  Is it a bird?

Yes, it is.

No, it isn't.

2. Complete the questions and write the answers.

1. <u>Is it a</u> snake?

   <u>Yes</u> , it is.

2. _____ _____ _____ owl?

   _____ , it isn't.

3. _____ _____ _____ spider?

   _____ , _____ _____ .

4. _____ _____ _____ fish?

   _____ , _____ _____ .

1. Write the missing letter.

1. A B C ____

2. G ____ I J

3. ____ L M N

4. Q R ____ T

5. W X ____ Z

2. Connect the dots. Trace and color.

Hello! I'm a _____ .

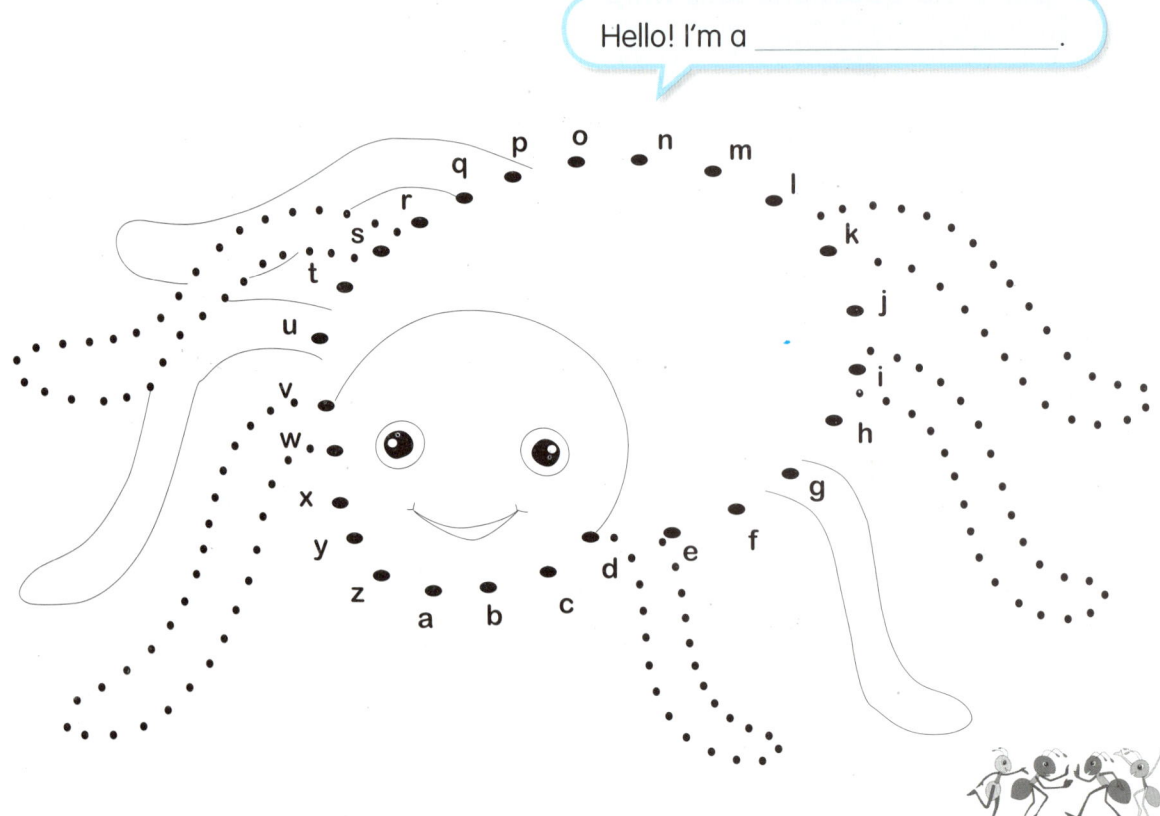

I can ...!

Name Pets

Look and write ✓ or ✗.

1. ☐ snake   ☐ spider

2. ☐ bird   ☐ owl

3. ☐ ant   ☐ lizard

4. ☐ cat   ☐ fish

5. ☐ mouse   ☐ dog

Talk about the Pets

Look at the previous exercise. Write sentences.

1. It isn't a snake.   It's a spider.

2. _____. _____.

3. _____. _____.

4. _____. _____.

5. _____. _____.

Ask and Answer about Pets

Match the questions and answers.

1.    What is it?   a) No, it isn't.

2.    Is it a mouse?   b) It's a fish.

3.    Is it an owl?   c) It's a snake.

4.   What is it?   d) Yes, it is.

Say the Letters of the Alphabet

Say these letters.

E   G   H   I   A   J   C   K   O   W

Unit
3

Do and Share!

Make a bookmark.

You need:

✓ construction paper

✓ crayons

✓ a pair of scissors

1. Trace.

2. Cut.

3. Color.

Lizard, lizard,
Help me look,
For the page,
In my book.

Go to Unit 3!

19

Unit 3 · The Cool School

Lesson 1

1. Find and number.

1. rulers	6. lunchboxes
2. pens	7. crayons
3. school bags	8. notebooks
4. books	9. computers
5. erasers	10. pencils

 1

2. Circle the correct word.

1.  book / books

2.  lunchbox / lunchboxes

3.  eraser / erasers

4.  pen / pens

5.  school bag / school bags

3. Unscramble the letters to make words. In your notebook, draw pictures to go with the words.

oycarns _____

rumpecots _____

elrrsu _____

skoentobo _____

scipnel _____

4. Look, say and spell.

1.

2.

3.

4.

5.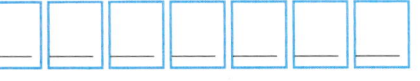

20

Lesson 2

1. Make the words plural.

1. crayon   _____crayons_____
2. school bag   _____
3. lunchbox   _____
4. eraser   _____
5. book   _____

6. pen   _____
7. notebook   _____
8. pencil   _____
9. computer   _____
10. ruler   _____

2. Circle the correct words. Correct the wrong sentences.

1.

They are / ~~aren't~~ school bags.

They are computers.

2.

They are / aren't pencils.

_____

3.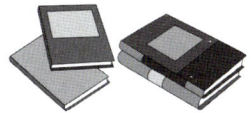

They are / aren't notebooks.

_____

4.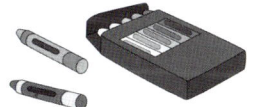

They are / aren't crayons.

_____

5.

They are / aren't lunchboxes.

_____

3. Look and complete.

What are they?

They're pencils.

What _____ _____?

_____ _____.

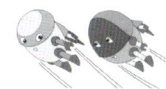

1. Unscramble the questions. Answer them with *Yes, they are* or *No, they aren't*.

1.

   rulers / ? / they / Are /

   Are they rulers?

   Yes, they are.

2.

   ? / they / snakes / Are /

   _____

   _____

3.

   dogs / Are / they / ? /

   _____

   _____

4.

   Are / rulers / ? / they /

   _____

   _____

2. Look and write questions and answers.

1.

   Are they spiders?

   Yes, they are.

2.

   _____

   _____

3.

   _____

   _____

Lesson 4

1. Read and color the correct number.

twenty	20	10	2
thirteen	3	13	15
seventeen	7	19	17
fourteen	14	4	13
sixteen	6	16	15

eleven	1	11	12
nineteen	18	9	19
fifteen	15	16	5
eighteen	8	17	18
twelve	12	11	2

2. Count and complete.

eleven snakes

I can ...!

Name School Supplies

Find eight words in the word snake.

sdlislycomputersschoolbagscrayonsnpepencilslunchboxesperpnerasersnotebookspensvm

Talk About School Supplies

Complete the sentences using *are* or *aren't*.

1. They _____ pens.

2. They _____ lizards.

3. They _____ ants.

4. They _____ notebooks.

5. They _____ pencils.

Ask and Answer About School Supplies

Color the correct question.

1. Yes, they are. | What are they? | Are they erasers? |

2. They're erasers. | What are they? | Are they erasers? |

Count From 11 to 20

Read and write the number.

1. sixteen   _____

2. eleven   _____

3. twenty   _____

4. fifteen   _____

5. eighteen _____

6. twelve   _____

Unit 4

Do and Share!

Make a Memory Game.

You need:

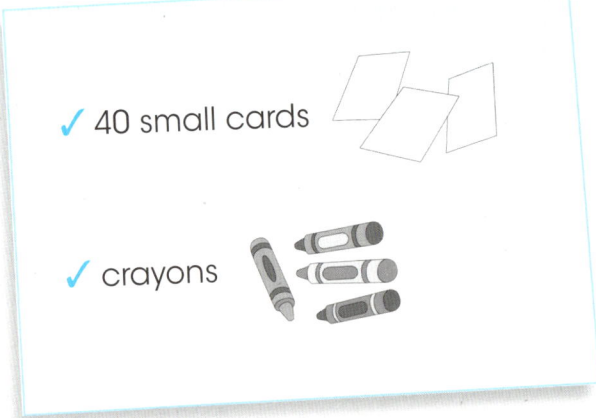

✓ 40 small cards

✓ crayons

1. Make pairs.

2. Play.

Look! Nine!

Go to Unit 4!

Unit 4 · The Toy Store

Lesson 1

1. Find and number.

1. doll	6. balloon
2. ball	7. train
3. plane	8. kite
4. car	9. dinosaur
5. boat	10. teddy bear

 ☐  ☐  ☐  1

 ☐  ☐  ☐  ☐

☐  ☐

2. Find 4 words with 4 letters in Exercise 1. Write them down.

_____

_____

_____

_____

3. Complete the words.

p __ __ n __   __ a __

__ __ ll __ o __   t r __ __ __

__ __ dd __   b __ __ r

__ __ __ __ s a __ __

4. Write the words in alphabetical order.

plane   kite   boat   doll   train   car

5. Look, say and spell.

1. ☐☐☐☐☐☐☐☐☐

4.  ☐☐☐

2. ☐☐☐☐

5.  ☐☐☐☐☐☐☐

3. 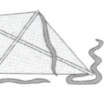 ☐☐☐☐

1. Write *S* for Singular or *P* for Plural.

1. mouse _____S_____   6. owls _____

2. lunchbox _____   7. computer _____

3. kites _____   8. teddy bears _____

4. dinosaurs _____   9. balloon _____

5. eraser _____   10. dogs _____

2. (Circle) *This* or *That*.

1.

(This) / That is a train.

2.

This / That is a balloon.

3.

This / That is a spider.

4.

This / That is a doll.

3. (Circle) *These* or *Those*.

1.

These / (Those) are boats.

2.

These / Those are ants.

3.

These / Those are cats.

4.

These / Those are teddy bears.

Lesson 3

1. Answer the questions.

1.

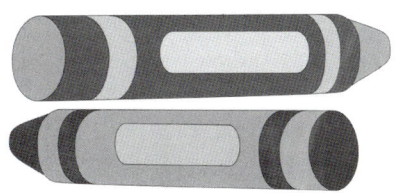

What are these?

<u>They're crayons</u>.

2.

What are those?

_____.

3.

What's this?

_____.

4.

_____.

2. Write questions for the answers.

1.

<u>What's that</u>?

It's a plane.

2.

_____?

They're teddy bears.

3.

_____?

It's a mouse.

4.

_____?

They're computers.

1. Play the "Flying High" Game.

You need:

A dice    A counter

1. Play with a friend.
2. Roll the dice. Say the word and spell it.
3. Finish the race first.
   Wrong = Miss a turn!

FINISH

eight

fifteen

eleven

twenty

three

twelve

nineteen

START

Lesson 5

I can ...!

Name Toys

Read and draw.

1. teddy bear

2. train

Complete using: *These*, *computer*, *What*, *snakes*, *those* and *that*.

1.

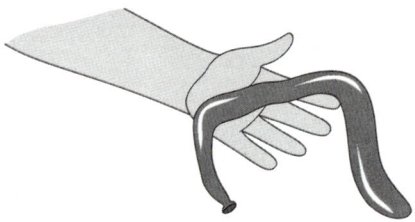

_____ is this?

It's a balloon.

2.

What are _____?

They're _____.

3.

What is _____?

It's a _____.

4.

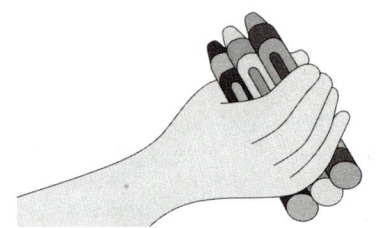

_____ are crayons.

Spell Words

Please, spell

_____

Please, spell

_____

Please, spell

_____

Unit
5

Do and Share!

Make an Alphabet Poster.

Draw, cut and paste on the construction paper.

You need:

✓ colored paper

✓ scissors

✓ a glue stick

✓ a large piece of construcion paper

Say the alphabet in English!

Please, spell cat.

Say the alphabet backwards!

Go to Unit 5!

The Attic

Unit 5

Lesson 1

1. Find and color.

1. purple	6. pink
2. white	7. brown
3. orange	8. yellow
4. green	9. red
5. black	10. blue

2. Find nine colors.

```
W D P U R P L E P B
H I G R E E N R I L
I Y E L L O W E N A
T B R O W N S D K C
E L B L U E Y O M K
```

Which color is missing? _____

3. How many …

colors start with P? _____

colors start with B? _____

colors start with G? _____

4. Choose a color and draw the circle. Spell the color.

Lesson 2

1. Read and color.

The teddy bear is brown.

The boats are red.

The plane isn't white. It's green.

The books are blue.

The pens aren't green. They're black.

The dog isn't brown. It's yellow.

The cats aren't green. They're pink.

The train isn't orange. It's purple.

2. Look and color. Complete the sentences.

| yellow | red | green | brown |

1. The kite _____ _____.

2. _____ dinosaurs _____ brown.

3. The car _____ red. It's _____.

4. The pencils _____ blue. _____.

1. Color according to the number.

one = green

two = yellow

three = brown

four = orange

five = blue

six = pink

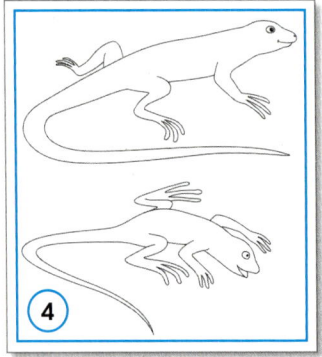

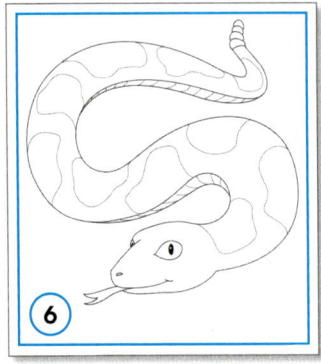

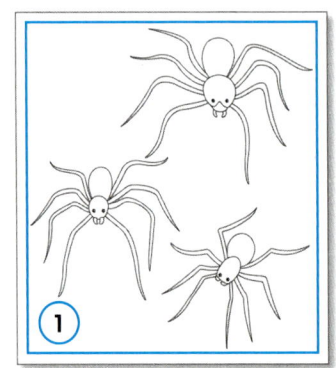

2. Look, read and match.

1. Are the spiders yellow?

2. Is the mouse yellow?

3. What color is the owl?

4. What color are the lizards?

5. Are the birds blue?

6. Is the snake orange?

Yes, it is.

They're orange.

No, it isn't.

Yes, they are.

No, they aren't.

It's brown.

Lesson 4

1. Look and label. Use the words in the box.

triangle   square   rectangle   circle   star

triangle

2. Read and write the letters.

A) Oh no!

B) Here you are.

C) Thanks.

D) Give me a rectangle, please.

I can ...!

Say the Colors

Follow the lines and color.

blue

purple

brown

yellow

green

red

pink

black

orange

white

Describe Animals and Things

1. Read and color.

Two green balloons.

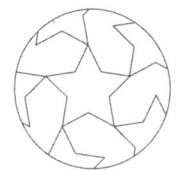

One yellow ball.

2. Write sentences.

The balloons aren't _____.   They're _____.

_____.   _____.

Ask and Answer about Colors

Look at the previous exercise.
Answer the questions.

1. What color are the balloons?

2. Is the ball yellow?

Name Shapes

Read and draw.

triangle

square

Ask for Things

Complete the dialogue. Use these words:
pen, *Thanks*, *Give* and *you*.

_____ me a _____, please.

Here _____ are.

_____.

Review
1

Do and Share!

Make a Mobile.

You need:

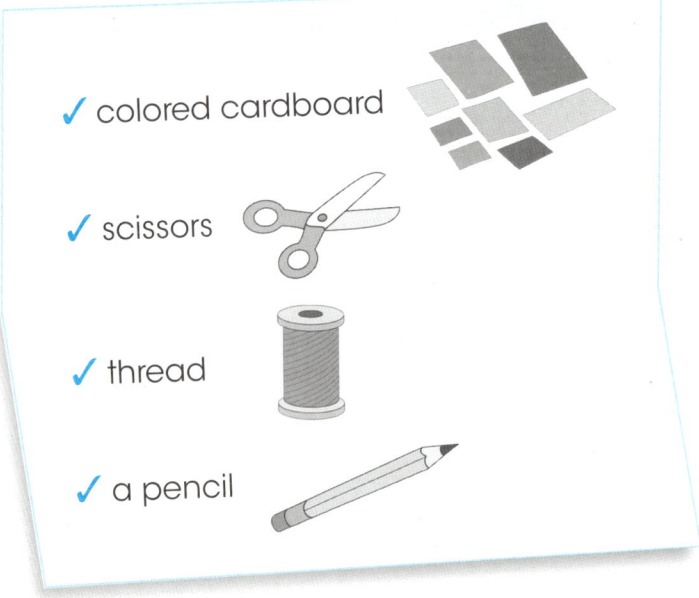

✓ colored cardboard

✓ scissors

✓ thread

✓ a pencil

1. Cut.

2. Attach a thread.

3. Tie the shapes to the pencil.

The stars are yellow. The triangle is blue. The circles aren't green. They're red.

Go to Review 1!

Review 1

1. (Circle) the word that doesn't belong.

1. eleven   eight   (cake)   fifteen   one

2. brown   pencil   ruler   pen   eraser

3. rectangle   plane   square   triangle   star

4. bird   snake   owl   cat   kite

5. balls   ant   books   dolls   dogs

6. blue   red   black   green   crayon

7. look   clap   listen   close   robot

2. Read and match.

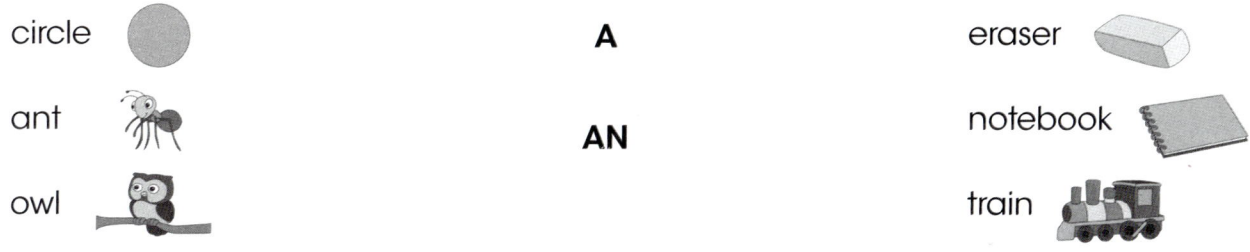

circle

ant

owl

A

AN

eraser

notebook

train

3. Correct the sentences.

1. It's a spider.   It isn't a spider.
   It's a fish.

2. They're kites.

3. It's a snake.

4. They're school bags.

5. It's a boat.

4. Write the correct question from the box for each answer.

> What color is the rectangle?   Is it a lizard?   What's your name?
>
> Are they computers?   How old is she?   What color are the stars?
>
> What's her name?   What is it?   How old are you?

1. _____.   It's a car.

2. _____.   My name's Pete.

3. _____.   They're blue.

4. _____.   I'm seven.

5. _____.   It's green.

6. _____.   Her name's Lulu.

7. _____.   No, they aren't.

8. _____.   She's nine.

9. _____.   Yes, it is.

5. Circle and color.

1.
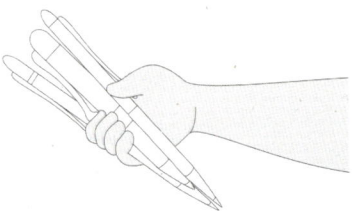
These / Those are pens.
They're yellow.

2.

This / That is a dinosaur.
It's brown.

3.

These / Those are balloons.
They're orange.

4.
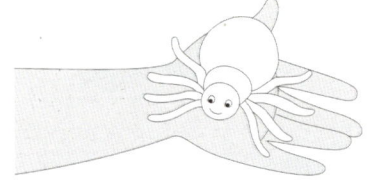
This / That is a spider.
It's green.

Go to Unit 6!

Unit 6 · The Tree House

Lesson 1

1. Find and number.

1. mirror	6. drawer
2. wall	7. clock
3. chair	8. shelf
4. box	9. lamp
5. bed	10. table

2. How many ants are there in the picture? _____

3. Guess the words.

l ___ ___ p

___ ___ l l

___ ___ x

c h ___ ___ ___

4. Number the words in alphabetical order.

☐ shelf		☐ bed	
☐ table		☐ mirror	
☐ clock		☐ drawer	

5. Look, say and spell.

1.  ☐ ☐ ☐ ☐ ☐ ☐

2.  ☐ ☐ ☐ ☐ ☐

3. ☐ ☐ ☐ ☐ ☐

4.  ☐ ☐ ☐

5.  ☐ ☐ ☐

1. Look and write *in, on* or *under*.

1. _____   2. _____   3. _____

2. Look at the picture for one minute.

3. Cover the picture and answer the questions in your notebook.

1. Where is the kite?
2. Where are the books?
3. Where are the spiders?
4. Where is the plane?

5. Where is the doll?
6. Where are the pens?
7. Where is the cat?
8. Where are the erasers?

How many points for you?

4. Check your answers. Give yourself one point for each correct answer.

5. Look at the picture again and write the question for the answer.

_____? It's under the table.

Lesson 3

1. Read and draw.

Draw five ants. They're on the chair.

Draw a mouse. It's under the bed.

Draw three spiders. They're on the wall.

Draw a cat. It's under the chair.

Draw two lizards. They're in the box.

Draw a dog. It's on the bed.

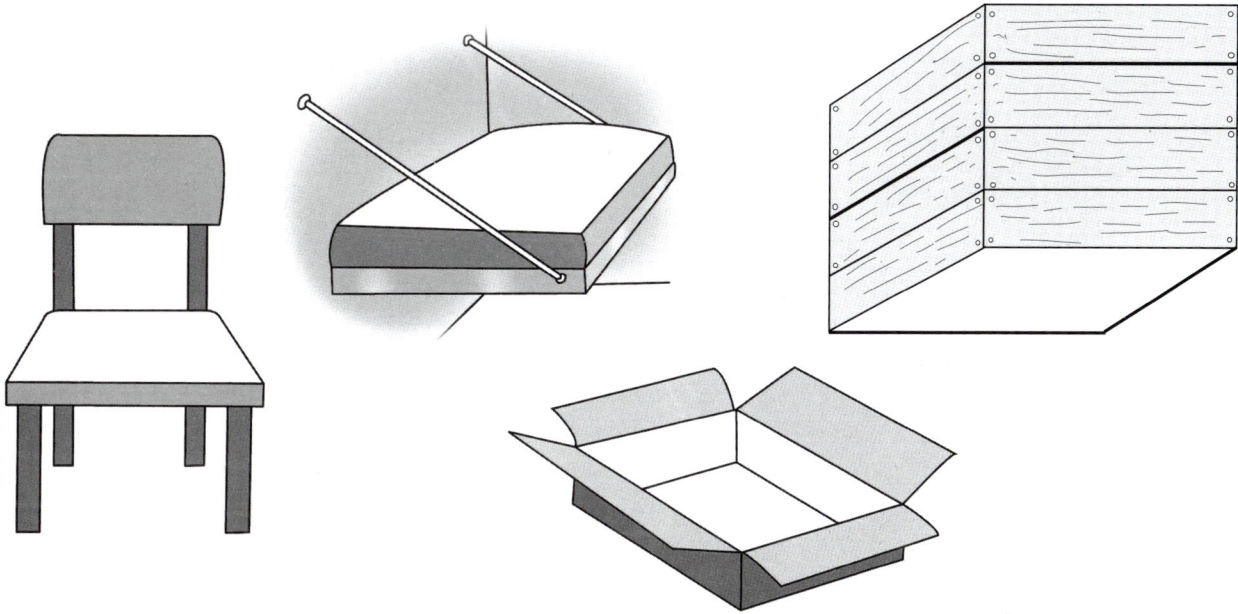

2. Unscramble the questions. Color the correct answers.

1. the / on / Is / cat / chair / the / ?

   | Yes, it is. | No, it isn't. |

2. ? / lizards / Are / in / the / the / box

   | Yes, they are. | No, they aren't. |

3. the / Is / ? / dog / the / on / chair

   | Yes, it is. | No, it isn't. |

4. bed / the / the / Is / ? / mouse / under

   | Yes, it is. | No, it isn't. |

5. box / ants / Are / in / the / ? / the

   | Yes, they are. | No, they aren't. |

6. are / ? / the / Where / spiders

   | They're on the wall. |

   | They're in the box. |

1. Complete the speech bubbles.

Don't sit down! | Don't touch that! | Don't eat that! | Don't jump!

Don't open that! | Don't throw trash! | Don't drink that!

Lesson 5

I can ...!

Name Furniture

Unscramble and draw.

orrmir	tlabe	occlk

_____

achir	mlap

_____

Use _in_, _on_ and _under_

Look and circle.

in / on / under   in / on / under   in / on / under

Talk and Ask About Where Things Are

Complete the questions and answers.

1. _____ the ball under the table?

   _____, _____ _____.

2. _____ is the ball?

   _____ shelf.

Give and Follow Negative Commands

Write the negative command.

_____

Do and Share!

Make a Home for Fred.

You can use your cutouts
on page 81.

You need:

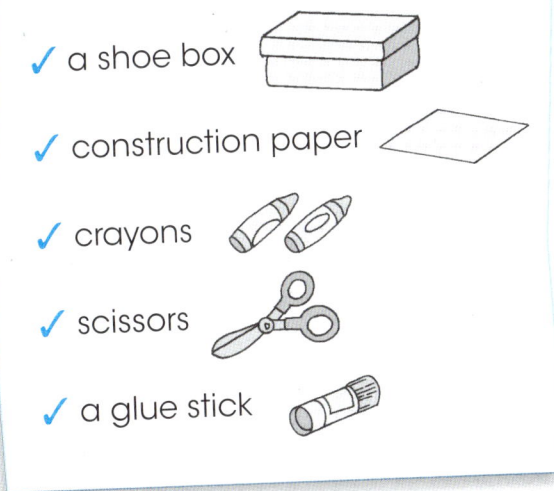

✓ a shoe box

✓ construction paper

✓ crayons

✓ scissors

✓ a glue stick

1. Trace and color.

2. Cut.

3. Glue.

The kite is on the bed and
the ball is under the bed.

Go to Unit 7

1. Find and number.

1. sweater	6. socks
2. dress	7. shirt
3. cap	8. skirt
4. shorts	9. hat
5. pants	10. shoes

2. How many words start with *sh*? Write them down in your notebook.

3. Which word appears first in the dictionary? _____

4. Complete the words.

so / ss / pa / er / sk / at

sweat ___ ___   ___ ___ cks   ___ ___ irt

dre ___ ___   h ___ ___   ___ ___ nts

5. Look, say and spell.

1. ▢ ▢ ▢
2. ▢ ▢ ▢ ▢ ▢
3. ▢ ▢ ▢

4. ▢ ▢ ▢ ▢ ▢
5. ▢ ▢ ▢ ▢ ▢

Lesson 2

1. Read and color.

My hat is red.
Your hat is blue.

Your shoes are green.
My shoes are orange.

2. Follow the lines and write sentences in your notebook.

sweater   red

pants   blue

dress   black

shoes   green

socks   purple

cap   white

His sweater is purple.

3. Complete the sentence with *our* and *their*. Unscramble and color the shirts.

_____ shirts are nagoer. _____ shirts are llwyeo.

1. Write the correct number in the speech bubbles.

1. The brown one.   3. It's on the table.

2. Where's the hat?   4. Which one?

2. Look and complete the conversation.

_____ are _____?

_____ ones?

_____.

They're _____.

Lesson 4

1. Read and match.

1. football player

2. doctor

3. police officer

4. dancer

5. pilot

2. Look and complete.

_____ do you _____ ?

I'm _____ _____.

football player

What

do

you

What do _____ do?

We're _____.

doctors

a

I can ...!

Name Clothes

Look. Tick ✓ or cross ✗.

 skirt ☐

 pants ☐

 cap ☐

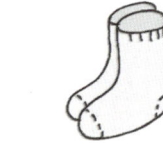 shoes ☐

dress ☐

 hat ☐

Use *my, your, his, her, our* and *their*

Look and match.

her
my
his
their

Use *Which*

Read and (circle) the correct words.

Where are the pen / pens?

Which one / ones?

The blue one / ones.

It's / They're in the drawer.

Ask and Answer About Jobs

Choose a job.
Draw your picture and answer the question.

doctor	pilot	dancer	police officer

What do you do? _____

Do and Share!

Make their clothes.

You need:

✓ paper

✓ a pencil

✓ scissors

✓ crayons

✓ Cut-out
TB p.259

1. Draw and color.

2. Cut.

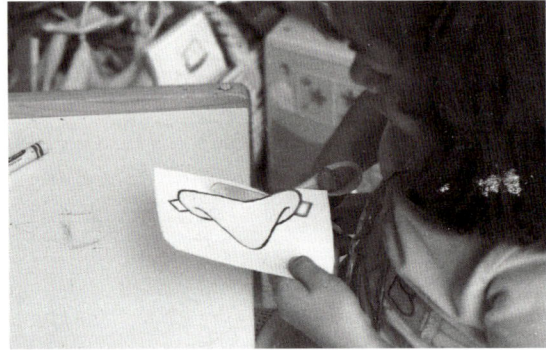

His hat is yellow. His pants and his shoes are red. Look! His shirt is white.

Go to Unit 8

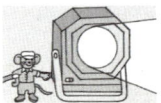

Unit 8 · The Park

Lesson 1

1. Find and number.

1. skateboard	6. roller skates
2. frisbee	7. helmet
3. racket	8. bat
4. scooter	9. sneakers
5. jump rope	10. bicycle

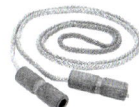  

□ □ □ □

□ □ □ □

 1

□ 1

2. Decode.

10/1/3/6/4/12

A = 1	L = 7
B = 2	M = 8
C = 3	O = 9
E = 4	R = 10
H = 5	S = 11
K = 6	T = 12

_____

11/3/9/9/12/4/10

_____

2/1/12

_____

5/4/7/8/4/12

_____

3. In your notebook, write the words in alphabetical order.

jump rope   skateboard   bicycle

roller skates   frisbee

4. Answer the questions.

How many balls? _____

How many vowels in *sneakers*? _____

5. Look, say and spell.

1.  □ □ □ □ □ □ □ □ □

2.  □ □ □

3.  □ □ □ □ □ □

4.  □ □ □ □ □ □

5. 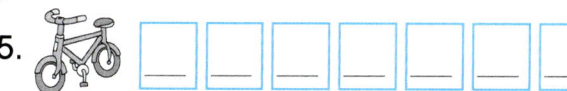 □ □ □ □ □ □ □

1. Look and color.

1 = red   2 = blue   3 = yellow   4 = green   5 = purple   6 = brown

2. <u>Underline</u> the correct sentences. Correct the wrong ones.

1. Adam's helmet is blue. _____.

2. Anita's sneakers are green. _____.

3. Betty's roller skates are red. _____.

4. Ben's scooter is purple. _____.

3. Use the words and write four more sentences.

1. Adam / bicycle   <u>Adam's bicycle is red</u>.

2. Anita / blue   _____.

3. Ben / yellow   _____.

4. Betty / frisbee   _____.

5. Adam / sneakers   _____.

Can you write two more sentences in your notebook?

Lesson 3

1. Look and answer the questions.

Kiko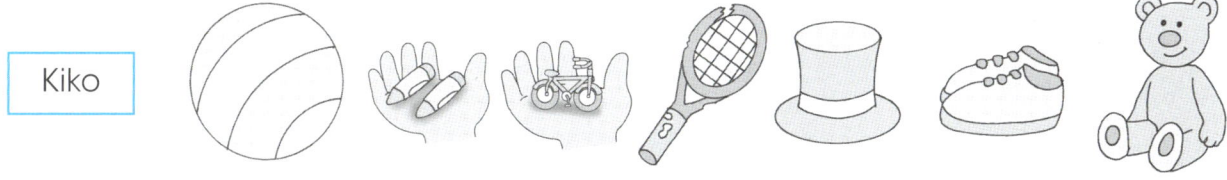

Velvet

1. Whose racket is this?

3. Whose teddy bear is that?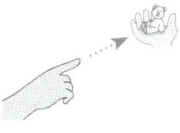

_____

2. Whose shoes are those?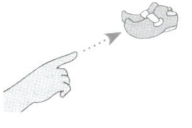

4. Whose crayons are these?

_____

2. Write questions for the answers.

1. _____?

They're Kiko's.

2. _____?

It's Velvet's.

3. _____?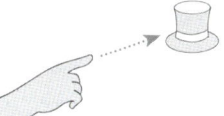

It's Kiko's.

4. _____?

They're Velvet's.

1. Complete the dialog and write it in order.

course

eraser

very

welcome

you

borrow

please

Thank you _____ much.

Can I _____ your _____, _____?

You're _____.

Yes, of _____. Here _____ are.

_____

_____

_____

_____

2. Circle the correct picture.

3. Read and do.

Draw a new kite. Color it blue.

Draw two old sneakers. Color them green.

Draw a big dinosaur. Color it black.

Draw a small car. Color it red.

Lesson 5

I can...!

Name Sports Equipment

Look and circle.

bat   racket   helmet

scooter   bicycle   skateboard

roller skates   frisbee   sneakers

Ask and Talk about Belongings

Complete the sentences.

_____ balloon _____ big.   Kate's _____ are _____.

Complete the question and answer it.

_____ _____ that?

_____ _____ _____.

Borrow and Lend Things

You need a ruler. What do you say to a friend?

_____

_____

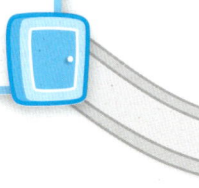

Unit
9

Do and Share!

Make a colorful crayon picture.

You need:

✓ paper

✓ crayons

✓ black ink

✓ a coin

1. Draw squares and color them.

2. Cover the squares with black ink.

3. Use a coin and draw a picture on the paper.

This is a boat and this is a fish.

Whose picture is that?

Go to Unit 9!

The Food Hall

Lesson 1

1. Find and number.

1. sandwich	6. hot dog
2. milkshake	7. donut
3. apple	8. banana
4. soda	9. cookie
5. hamburger	10. orange

  [1]

2. Complete the puzzle.

H _ _ D _ _ _ S _ _ _ _ _ _ _ T _

_ _ _ K _ H _ _ _ _ _ _ _ _ G _ _

_ _ M _ _ R _ _ _ _ _ _ _ E _

_ _ _ W _ _ _ _ B _ _ _ _ _ _

_ O O _ _ _

3. (Circle) the word that comes first.

orange / sandwich   donut / apple   cookie / banana   hamburger / soda

4. Look, say and spell.

1. _ _ _ _

2.  _ _ _ _ _

3.  _ _ _ _ _ _ _

4.  _ _ _ _ _ _

5. 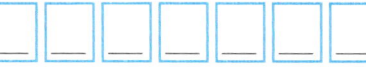 _ _ _ _ _ _ _ _ _

64

Lesson 2

1. Choose six things for your tray. (Circle) them.

2. What do you have? Color the correct words.

1. I [have] / [don't have] a sandwich.

2. I [have] / [don't have] a banana.

3. I [have] / [don't have] a hamburger.

4. I [have] / [don't have] a soda.

5. I [have] / [don't have] a cookie.

6. I [have] / [don't have] an apple.

3. Write four sentences. Use the words in the box.

| hot dog   orange   milkshake   donut |

1. _____ .

2. _____ .

3. _____ .

4. _____ .

1. Read, unscramble and answer. Use *Yes, I do.* or *No, I don't.*

1. Do you have a ogd _____ ?   _____

2. Do you have two elrrus _____ ?   _____

3. Do you have one npilec _____ ?   _____

4. Do you have a teki _____ ?   _____

5. Do you have a olalnob _____ ?   _____

2. Look and write five questions to ask a friend.

1. _____ ?

2. _____ ?

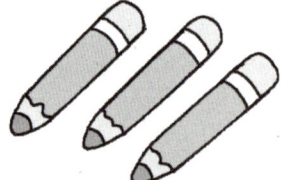

3. _____ ?

4. _____ ?

5. _____ ?

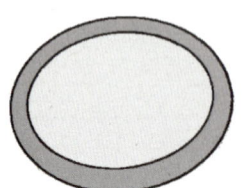

Lesson 4

1. Look and match.

1. $2 + $10 = [ ]

2. $5 + $5 = [ ]

3. $2 + $2 + $2 + $2 = [ ]

4. $5 + $1 = [ ]

5. $2 + $5 = [ ]

6. $5 + $5 + $5 + $5 = [ ]

a) $10.00

b) $7.00

c) $20.00

d) $6.00

e) $12.00

f) $8.00

2. Look, read and circle the correct word.

1.

I'm hungry / thirsty.

2.

Can I have a sandwich / soda, please?

3.

Of course. That's two / twelve dollars, please.

I can ...!

Name Food

Complete the words.

n/u/o   d __ __ __ t

b/n/n   __ a __ a __ a

w/h/s   __ and __ i c __

p/e/p   a __ __ l __

Talk about What I Have

Complete the sentences. Use *have* or *don't have*.

I _____ a computer.

I _____ a doll.

I _____ a cat.

I _____ a bicycle.

Ask What People Have

Unscramble the question and ask it to a friend.

have / Do / a / skateboard / ? / you

_____

Buy Food

You are hungry. You want a hamburger. What do you say?

_____?

Draw.

Do and Share!

Make a pencil holder.

You need:

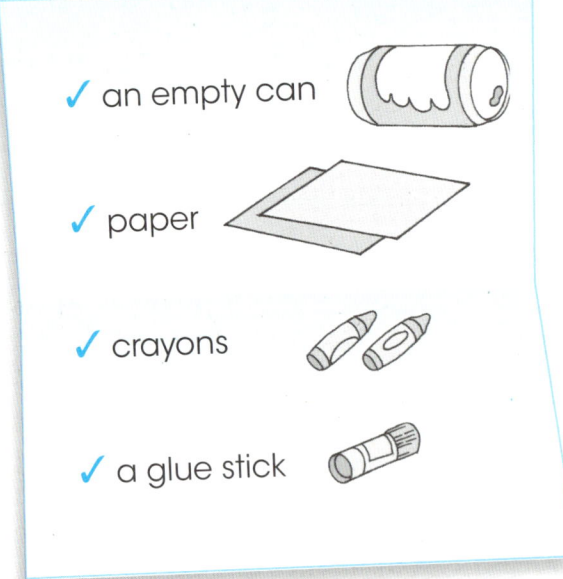

✓ an empty can

✓ paper

✓ crayons

✓ a glue stick

1. Write your name on the paper.

2. Stick the paper around the can.

3. Put your school supplies in your pencil holder.

This is my pencil holder. I have a pencil, a ruler and a pen.

Go to Unit 10!

1. Find and number.

1. head	6. nose
2. eyes	7. hands
3. arms	8. mouth
4. feet	9. ears
5. hair	10. legs

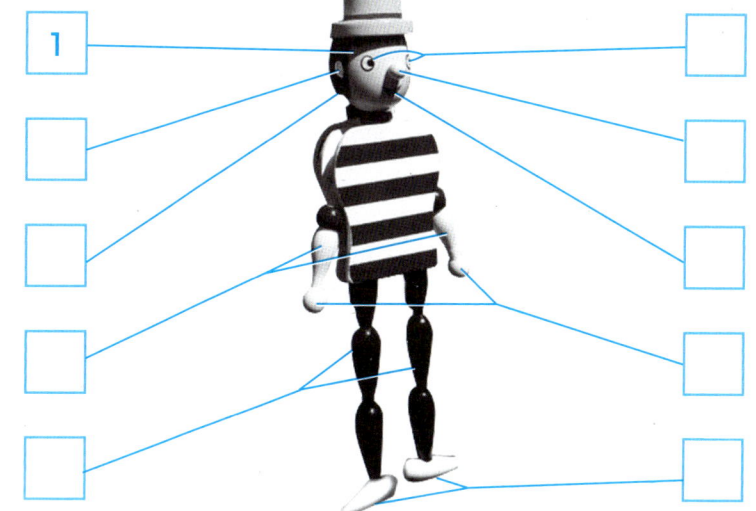

2. Unscramble the letters and write the words.

ahir _____

saer _____

snahd _____

eeys _____

tmuoh _____

3. Number in alphabetical order.

legs ☐

head ☐

arms ☐

nose ☐

feet ☐

4. Play Simon says …

5. Look, say and spell.

1. 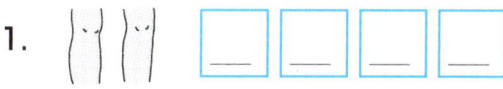 ☐ ☐ ☐ ☐

2.  ☐ ☐ ☐ ☐

3.  ☐ ☐ ☐ ☐

4.  ☐ ☐ ☐ ☐ ☐

5.  ☐ ☐ ☐ ☐

1. Color the puppet.

1 = orange

2 = blue

3 = pink

4 = purple

5 = brown

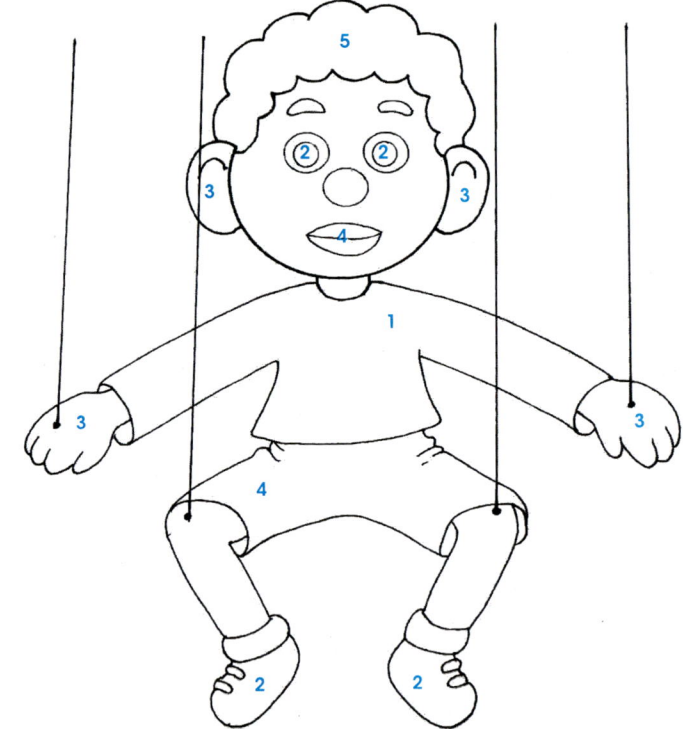

2. Complete the sentences.

| doesn't have |

1. This puppet _____ blue _____.

| doesn't have |

2. It _____ _____ orange hair.

| pink |

3. It has _____ ears.

| purple |

4. This puppet _____ long arms.

| has / eyes |

5. It _____ _____ a small head.

| has |

6. It has a _____ mouth.

3. Tick ✓ the correct sentences. Correct the wrong ones.

1. This puppet has big hands. _____

2. It has short arms. _____

3. This puppet has red hair. _____

4. It has a small head. _____

5. It has big feet. _____

6. It has long legs. _____

Lesson 3

1. What does Yoyo have? Follow the lines and answer the questions.

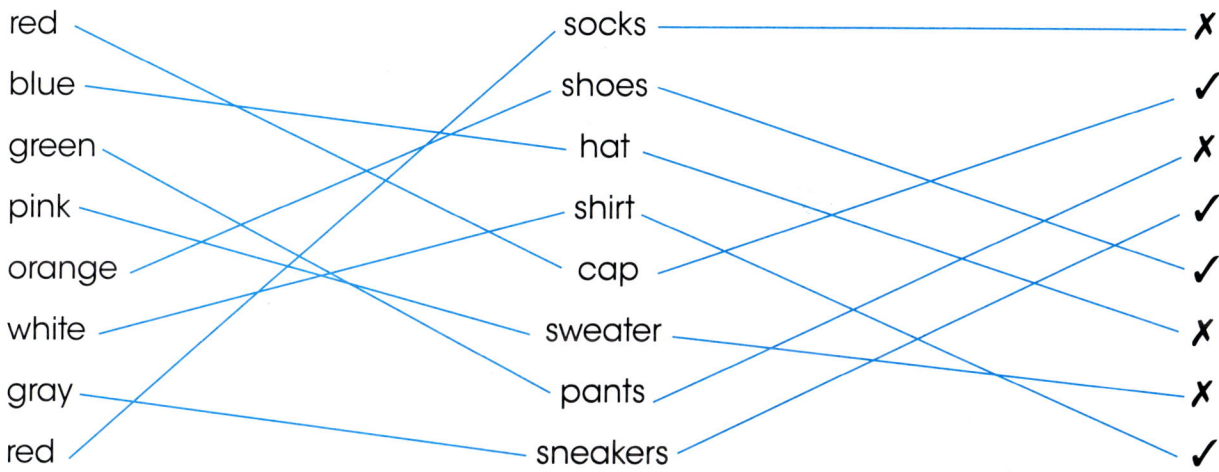

red

blue

green

pink

orange

white

gray

red

socks ——— ✗

shoes ——— ✓

hat ——— ✗

shirt ——— ✓

cap ——— ✓

sweater ——— ✗

pants ——— ✗

sneakers ——— ✓

1. Does Yoyo have a white shirt? <u>Yes</u>

2. Does Yoyo have a blue hat? _____

3. Does Yoyo have a pink sweater? _____

4. Does Yoyo have a red cap? _____

5. Does Yoyo have red socks? _____

2. Write questions for the answers.

1. _____?

Yes, he does. Yoyo has gray sneakers.

2. _____?

No, he doesn't. He doesn't have green pants.

3. _____?

No, he doesn't. He doesn't have red socks.

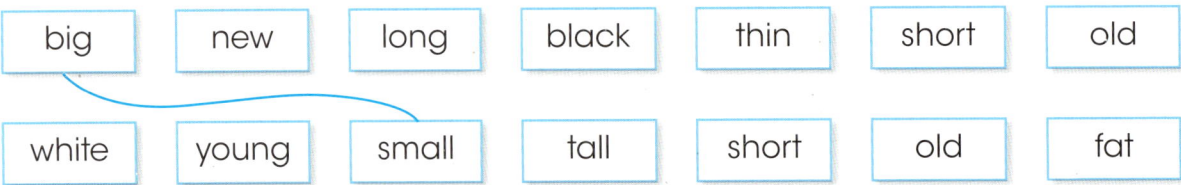

1. Match the opposites.

big	new	long	black	thin	short	old

white	young	small	tall	short	old	fat

2. Read and write the letter.

a) This puppet is old.

b) This puppet has long arms.

c) This puppet isn't short. He is tall.

d) This puppet has a big head.

e) This puppet isn't thin. He is fat.

3. Draw and color your puppet. Write about it.

_____

_____

_____

Lesson 5

I can...!

Name the Parts of the Body

Draw a mask with a long nose, big eyes, big ears and long hair.

Describe Physical Appearance

Change the sentences as in the example.

He has black hair.   She has green eyes.

He doesn't have black hair .   She _____ .

Does he have black hair ____?   _____ ?

He has a big nose.

_____ big nose.

_____ ?

Ask What People Have

Find the answer to the question.

Does your teacher have a dog?

_____

Use Adjectives

What's the opposite of *tall*?

_____

What's the opposite of *small*?

_____

What's the opposite of *fat*?

_____

Review
2

Do and Share!

Make puppets for LET'S HELP HENRY!

Use the cutouts on pages 83 and 85.

You need:

✓ crayons

✓ scissors

✓ sticky tape

Use a shoe box to make your theater.

Color the box and paste your puppets.

Today! Let's Help Henry!

Go to Review 2!

Review 2

1. Write the words where they belong. Add two more words to each column.

Furniture	Clothes	Sports Equipment	Food
_____	_____	_____	_____
_____	_____	_____	_____
_____	_____	_____	_____
_____	_____	_____	_____
_____	_____	_____	_____

scooter	nose	**Parts of the body**	bat	mouth
dress	cookie	_____	pants	shirt
head	helmet	_____	chair	hot dog
sweater	shelf	_____	racket	arms
bed	apple	_____	donut	drawer

2. Correct the sentences.

1.  The lamp is on the table.

   The lamp isn't on the table. It's on the chair.

2.  Her balloons are big.

   _____

3.  Rick's bicycle is big.

   _____

78

4.  I have three hot dogs.

_____

5.  He has small eyes.

_____

6. The mouse is on the bed.

_____

7. Lana is under the skateboard.

_____

3. Draw lines to make questions.

1. Does she   are these?

2. Are the apples in   is that?

3. Do you have   do you do?

4. Whose racket   on the shelf?

5. What do   have long hair?

6. Whose sneakers   the box?

7. What   you have?

8. Is the clock   a soda?

4. Match the answers to the questions in Exercise 3.

1. _Is the clock on the shelf_ ? Yes, it is.

2. _____ ? It's Karl's.

3. _____ ? No, I don't.

4. _____ ? Yes, she does.

5. _____ ? I have a hamburger.

6. _____ ? I'm a pilot.

7. _____ ? They're Sandra's.

8. _____ ? No, they aren't.

You've Finished Gateway 1!

Cutouts

Unit 6 (page 49)

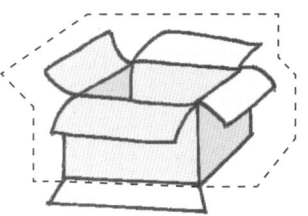

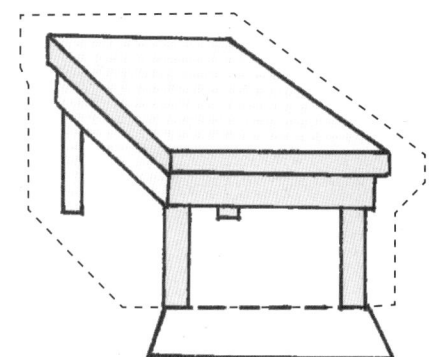

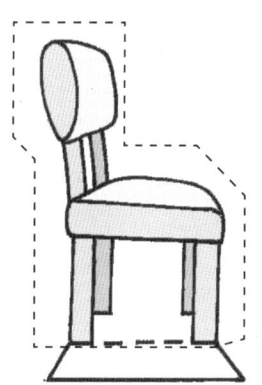

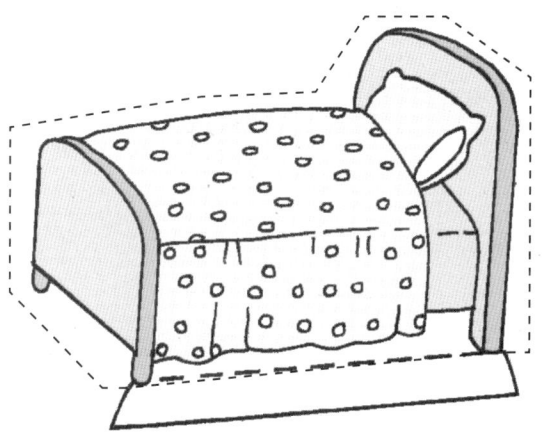

Unit 10 (page 77)

Henry

Friend 1

Friend 2

Police Officer

Unit 19 (page 77)

Unit 10 (page 77)

Doctor

Mother

Snowy

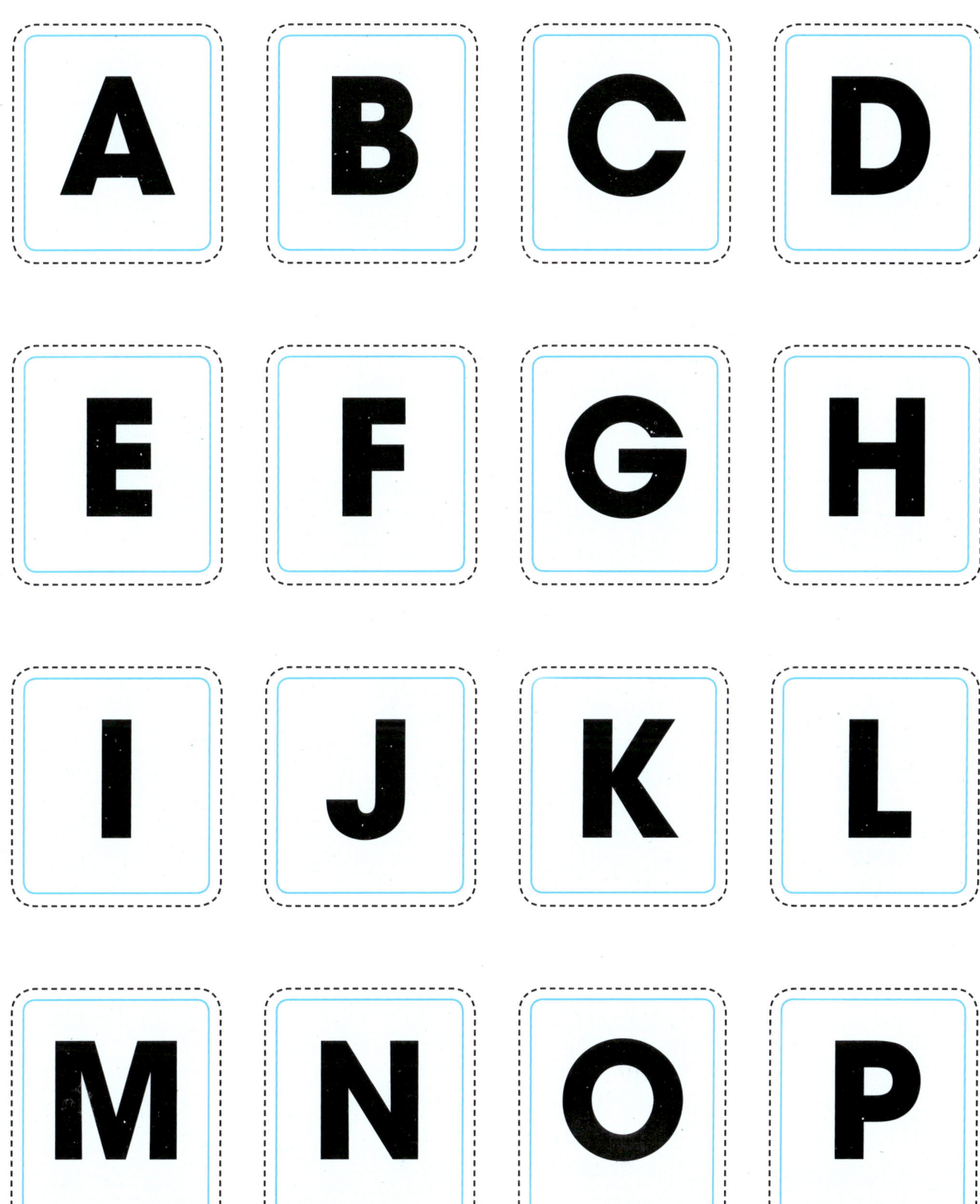

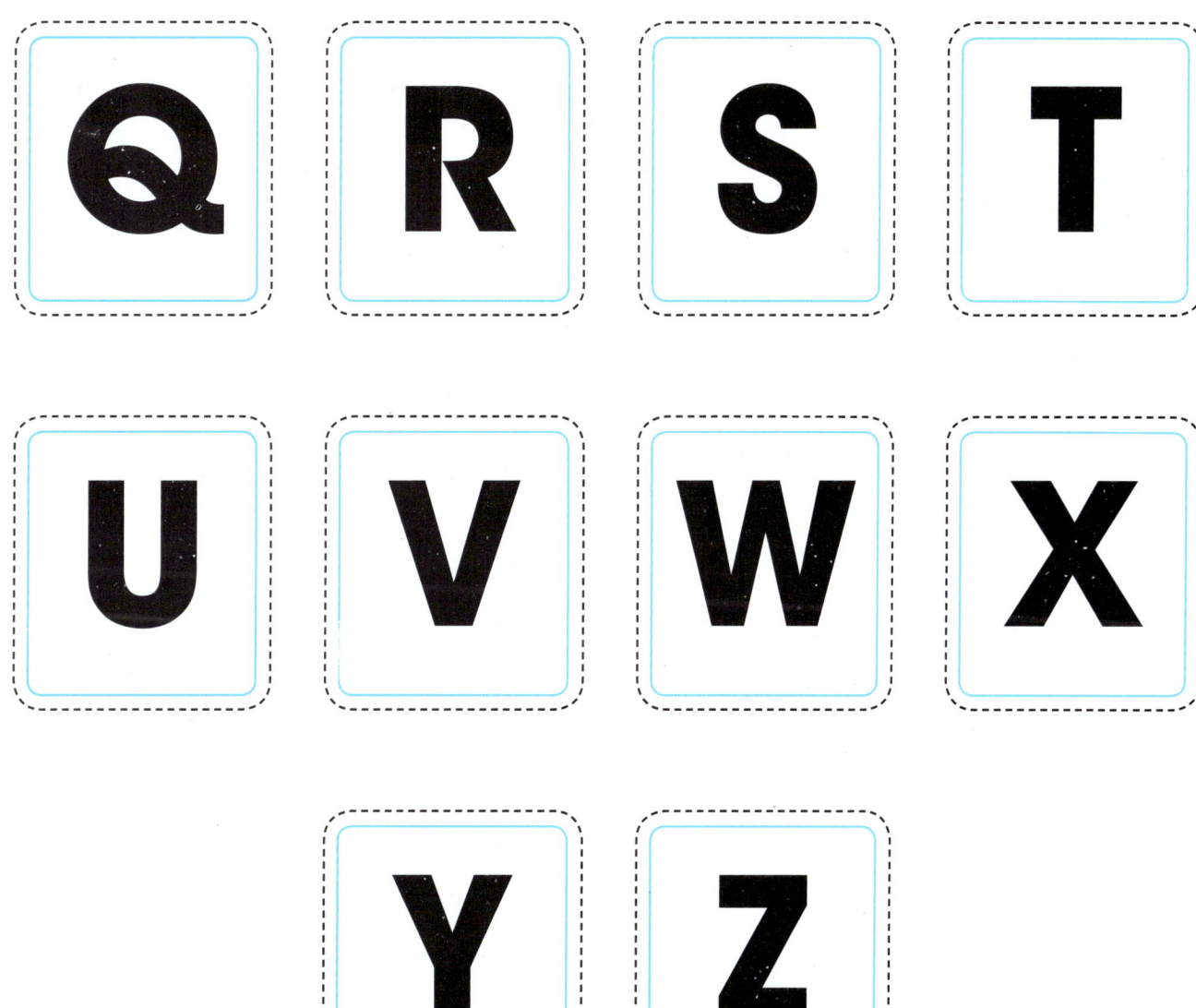

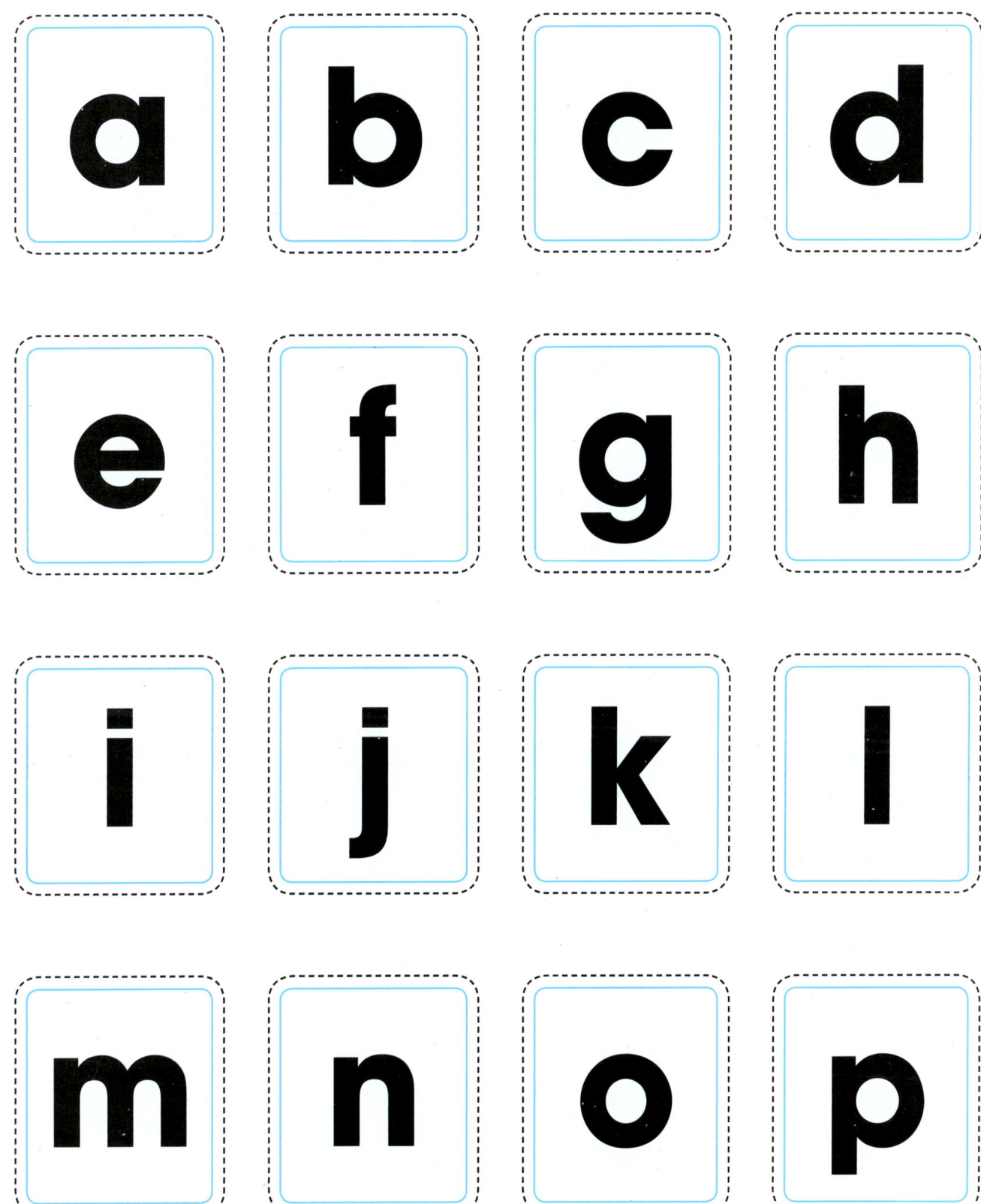

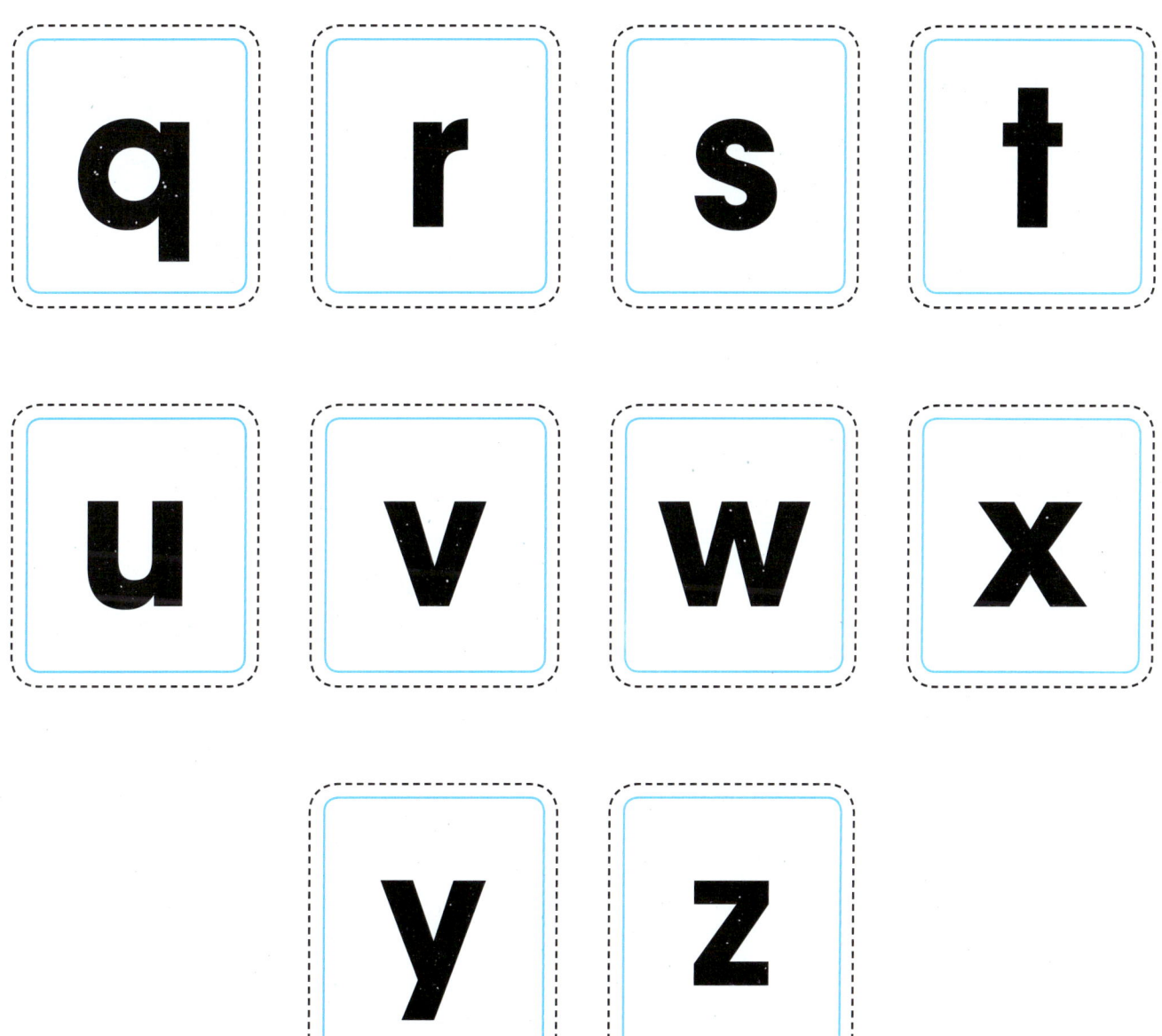

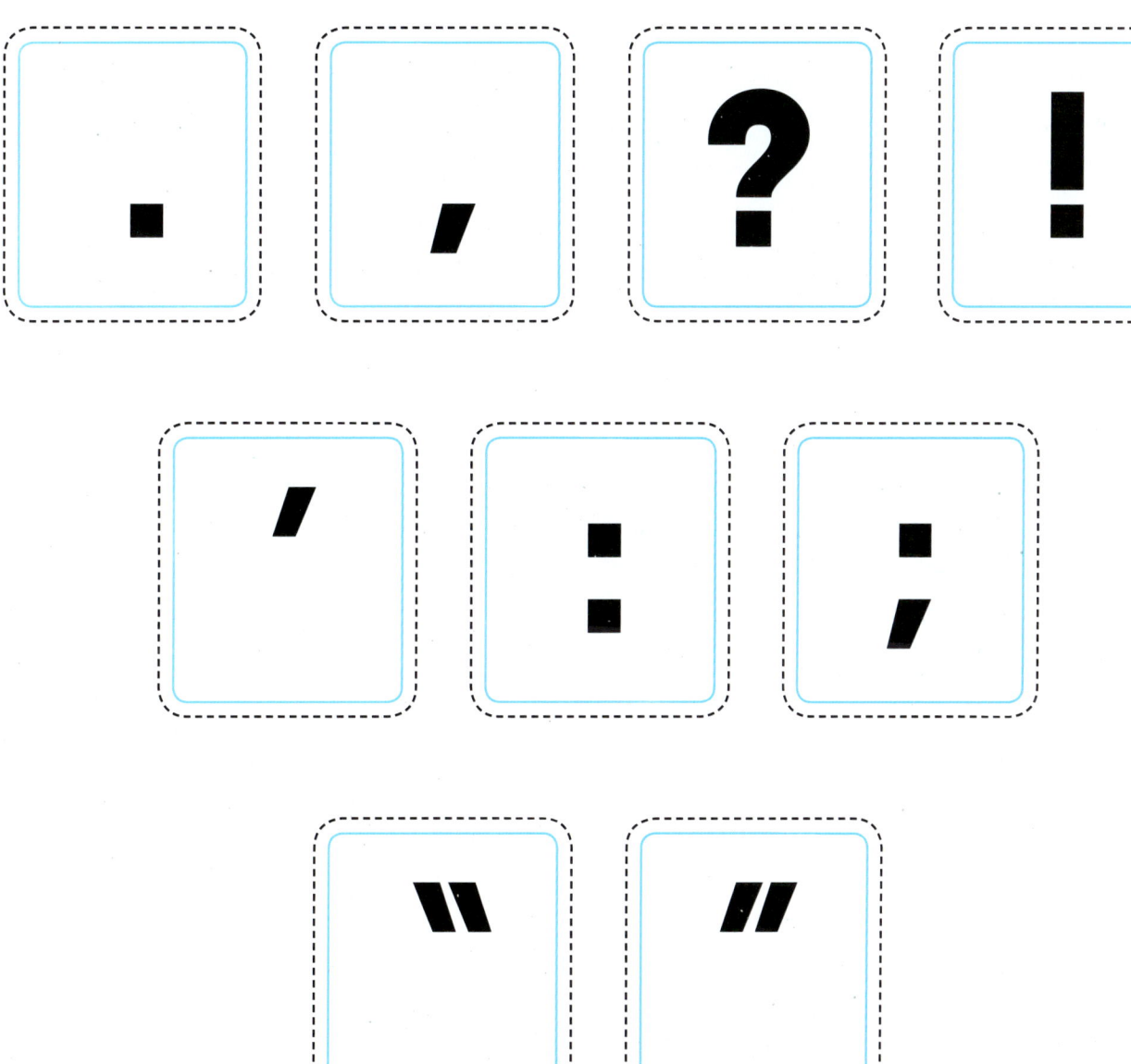